8972

Mat. #90021

W9-AZB-830

purchase Smart Apple $16.95 2001

Gangs and Violence

Perspectives on Violence

by Gus Gedatus

Consultant:
Jah-Rel Muata Kiongozi
Director of Youth Services
National Crime Prevention Council
Washington, DC

LifeMatters
an imprint of Capstone Press
Mankato, Minnesota

8972

LifeMatters Books are published by Capstone Press
PO Box 669 • 151 Good Counsel Drive • Mankato, Minnesota 56002
http://www.capstone-press.com

Printed in the United States of America

Library of Congress Cataloging-in-Publication Data
Gedatus, Gustav Mark.
     Gangs and violence / by Gus Gedatus.
          p.   cm. — (Perspectives on violence)
     Includes bibliographical references and index.
     Summary: Describes what gangs are, how they develop, how they create problems with their violent actions, and how to deal with them.
     ISBN 0-7368-0423-4 (book) — ISBN 0-7368-0439-0 (series)
     1. Gangs—United States—Juvenile literature. 2. Juvenile delinquency—United States—Juvenile literature. 3. Violence—United States—Juvenile literature. [1. Gangs. 2. Violence.] I. Title. II. Series
     HV6439.U5 G43 2000
     366.1´06´60973—dc21

                                        99-049268
                                      CIP

Staff Credits
Charles Pederson, editor; Adam Lazar, designer; Jodi Theisen, photo researcher

Photo Credits
Cover: The Stock Market/©Chuck Savage, large; Visuals Unlimited/©Jim Thompson, small
FPG International/©Ron Chapple, 55
International Stock/©Tom O'Brien, 8; ©John Neubauer, 43; ©Patric Ramsey, 48
Jim West/©Jim West, 54
Photo Network/©Grace Davies, 9; ©Jeffry W. Myers, 46; ©Eric R. Berndt, 53
Unicorn/©A. Ramey, 17, 19; ©Marie Mills/David Cummings, 20; ©Jim Shippee, 29; ©Tom McCarthy, 58
Uniphoto/35; ©Llewellyn, 7, 42; ©Mark Reinstein, 11, 27; ©Jack Mellott, 36; ©Bob Daemmrich Photos, 38

Table of Contents

A gang is an association of peers. Gangs form for many reasons.

Gangs have existed throughout much of history. Today's gangs use different methods from gangs in the past. However, there is no one type of gang or gang member.

People join gangs to have needs met that their families, schools, or communities aren't meeting.

Gang members mostly wait for something exciting to happen. Gangs may fight other gangs. Gang members sometimes fight each other, too.

Gang members may have certain traits.

Chapter 1

What Are Gangs All About?

What Is a Gang?

A gang is a self-formed association of peers. It may have many members, or only two or three. Gangs sometimes form because there are few other opportunities for the members. Some gangs may form because of hatred directed at the members because of their race. Gangs often have a structure, active members, and new recruits. Some gangs have rules that must be memorized. Gangs may hold meetings during which they read from books and discuss gang business. In many cases, gangs participate as a group in illegal activity. Members range in age from 8 to 30, but most are young adults.

All-female gangs sometimes form because of the poor way male gang members treat them. Female gangs are usually difficult for law enforcement to track.

Gangs From Past to Present

Gangs have existed for hundreds of years. As early as the 1500s, William Shakespeare wrote about gangs in his plays. By 1791, Philadelphia was trying to cope with young people who were causing problems. By 1825, New York City had gangs. Gangs of the 1920s were involved in gambling and bootlegging, which is illegally producing and selling alcohol. These gangs also were involved in extortion, or cheating people out of money. They also were involved in prostitution, which is selling sex for money.

By 1980, about 1,000 known gangs were in 300 cities in the United States. The number of members was about 50,000. By 1995, however, 23,000 gangs had more than 650,000 members. Experts believe that growing and spreading cities, better transportation, and widespread drug sales have spurred this increase.

In some ways, today's gangs are different from gangs of the past. Throughout history, the poorest or least respected people in society often have formed gangs. This is still true. However, there are other kinds of gangs today. Gangs may control large sums of money from illegal drug traffic, gun sales, and prostitution. Some gangs use modern communication devices such as cell phones. They might have automatic weapons.

However, gangs fit no stereotype. A stereotype is an overly simple opinion about a person, group, or thing. For example, some gangs don't commit violence. Some hate gangs may blend into the rest of society.

Why Do People Join Gangs?

People join gangs for many reasons. Some youths join gangs for a sense of having a family. They may come from a home in which the family doesn't function well. These youths may not value themselves highly. They may have other needs that their family or community doesn't meet. Some people join gangs because it's what the family does. Parents and even grandparents may have belonged to the same gang.

Such gangs may recruit people who feel separated from family or friends. These young people may feel good in the gang because their family or community has neglected them.

People from certain racial or cultural groups may feel powerless or without opportunities. They may not feel that they are a part of society. Gang membership can give young people a sense of belonging in some shared activity. They may think that the gang is cool. Youths may form or join a gang because people fear it. This fear can give members a feeling of power.

Poverty sometimes influences gang membership. Young people who grow up in poverty may struggle for a better life. Good jobs may not seem to be available to them. These young people may think joining a gang that is involved in crime is a good way to earn cash.

In many cases, gangs choose to move into communities that are unfamiliar with gang activity.

Common Gang Activities and Violence

The main activity of gangs is hanging out. They may feel bored while waiting for something to happen, so they look for something to do. Some gang activities are violent, including drug dealing, extortion, robbery, theft, and the intentional setting of fires. These activities may include physical violence.

Destruction of public and private property, also called vandalism, is another common gang activity. For example, gang members often leave gang graffiti behind to show their presence. This illegal drawing or writing on a surface has been called the newspaper of the streets. Gang members' graffiti gives messages to each other and to rival gangs. Abandoned houses, highways, and sidewalks often are targets for graffiti. Graffiti may be the first sign that a gang has arrived in a new community.

Gangs may want control over everything so they feel they have power. One way to have control and power is by getting a negative reputation. Activities that may earn a negative reputation include the use of bullying, threats, or other violence. Gang members may frighten witnesses or victims into not reporting a crime.

"Violence is part of life out there. In our area you see violence all the time. Either you stay ready, or it's going to get you."
—Mitchell, age 20, member of a drug gang

Much of gang life centers on getting what members call respect. Protecting the gang's honor or the gang's area may cause violence between gangs. Revenge on another gang may be another cause of violence. Sometimes gangs fight each other just because they always have. Members may not even know what the original disagreement was.

Gang violence may occur within gangs, too. Male gang members may fight over females. Gang members might argue about their status, or position, within a gang. One member may feel that another member has behaved disrespectfully toward him or her. Such conflicts within a gang may lead to fights, drive-by shootings, or even murder.

Traits of Gang Members

It is not accurate to say that gangs or gang members are all the same. Most gangs are different from one another. Yet some of the following traits apply to many people in gangs. Gang members may:

Feel neglected

Be young males; however, the number of all-female gangs is growing

Have seen alcohol or other drugs abused at home

Do poorly in school; however, many gang members are excellent students and may be involved in sports or other school activities

Live with only one parent or a grandparent

Be known for fighting during their early teens

Often be absent from school

Be poor; some gangs, however, do have money

Belong to the same race or ethnic group as the other members

Before they join a gang, members usually don't have higher rates of criminal behavior than nongang members. When members leave a gang, their activities usually are legal.

CHARLENE, AGE 14

Charlene and her friends love to swim on most warm summer days. The nearby public pool usually is not crowded. They often meet there.

One afternoon at the pool, Charlene and her friends heard a car pull into the parking lot. A group of guys got out. Seven other boys were walking toward the pool from the far side of the park.

At the first shot, people started screaming and running. Charlene pulled her friends off their towels and into the pool. The shooting continued. Charlene and her friends stayed in the pool until they heard sirens. Then the shooting stopped.

Females usually make up about 10 percent of any gang. Some females are forced to sell their body for sex. The gang abandons many females who become pregnant.

Points to Consider

Why do you think some people join gangs?

How do you feel about the use of force or violence in gangs?

How different do you think today's gangs are from those of the past? Explain.

Are there gangs in your city or area? If so, what do you think are some of their activities?

The gang way of life involves attitudes and beliefs. Many of these beliefs are negative. The gang way of life usually includes claiming a territory.

Some gangs have stages of membership. Gangs also may have their own symbols.

Police pressures have forced many gangs to be more creative in the way they dress. Clothing isn't always a good way to identify gang members.

There are many kinds of gangs. Some examples are East and West coast gangs, Asian gangs, and Spanish-speaking gangs.

Chapter **2**

Inner-City Gangs

The Gang Way of Life

Gangs may have certain beliefs or attitudes. These attitudes and beliefs may be called the gang way of life. For example, members are expected to be extremely loyal to the gang. They may believe that the gang is more important than anything. They often will do whatever the gang demands.

The gang way of life may not be too different from the daily life of some members. Every day, they may see violence or alcohol or other drug abuse. Theft and child abuse may be common in their life. For these people, the gang way of life simply continues the violence.

Myth: Gangs usually battle gangs of a different race.

Fact: Most gang conflict takes place among gangs of the same race or culture.

JUBE MAN, AGE 17

Jube Man had been in the Vipers gang since he was 15. His real name was Henry. The gang started calling him Jube Man because of some candy he liked. He didn't mind because he thought Henry was a stupid name.

For two years, Jube Man took part in many gang activities. He had never been arrested, although authorities questioned him once or twice. Last week he was part of an attack on a rival gang. Now he was preparing for revenge from that group. He carried a gun in his coat.

As Jube Man was leaving the apartment, his mother grabbed the gun. He fought to get the gun away from her as his little brother, Ralph, stood nearby. Before he knew what happened, the gun went off. Little Ralph lay on the floor in a pool of blood. Their mother started screaming and running around the apartment. Jube Man's sister called 9-1-1.

Jube Man couldn't fight back his tears. "I'm sorry, man," he cried. But when the paramedics came, little Ralph had already died.

The gang way of life can draw gang members together. They usually clearly understand individual roles and responsibilities. For example, gangs may have leaders and a clear chain of command. If a member fails to do a task, he or she may receive a "V" code. This means the member has violated a rule. The member may risk being beaten by the gang.

A local territory often is important to the gang way of life. The territory may be called a hood, gang turf, or barrio, the Spanish name for neighborhood. Gangs often choose names tied to their turf, such as the 18th Avenue Gang. Some names are chosen because they sound frightening or powerful.

Beliefs of Gang Members

Gang members may develop negative beliefs about how to fit in with their gang or in society. Gang members may believe any of the following:

They may believe in their gang, sometimes called a set or crew. This belief includes the illegal activities that the gang might do.

They may believe the end justifies the means. If an action gets something for the gang, then it's not important who the action may hurt.

In Canada, 15 out of every 100 young people arrested for illegal gang activities are females.

They may believe life is bad, so nothing matters.

They may believe in pleasure and in living for the present. Most gang members are hurt, dead, or in jail within three to eight years of joining. This contributes to the belief that only the present matters.

They may believe they are at war with other groups. They may feel no one is innocent in this war.

They may believe that their race is better than others. For example, they may believe whites are better than American Indians. They may hate people who belong to other races.

They may believe in Allah or God. These beliefs often are shallow and don't follow the real teachings of Allah or God.

They may believe in their gang's colors or style of dress.

Stages of Gang Membership

Gangs may have several stages of membership. For example, in the first stage, the gonnabee or wannabee wants to become a member. In another stage, the peripheral hangs around gang members but can't participate in activities. In another stage, the affiliate or gangbanger becomes a full gang member. Finally, hard-core members live only for the gang.

In some Spanish-speaking gangs, young members may be called peewees or lil winos. Members who live to be about 20 are called veteranos. They may take part in crimes, but often they only advise younger members. They might help to hide members, dispose of guns, and arrange meetings or parties.

Members usually move from one stage of membership to the next. New recruits may be expected to fight present members to show their worthiness. This may be called courting or jumping in. Their early activity may involve flashing gang signs and writing graffiti to claim turf. Extremely violent gangs may expect new members to take part in rape, drive-by shootings, or murder.

Shoo-Bo had been trying to get into the Bad Dogs gang since he

was 14. He had done many favors for gang members and worked hard to prove his worthiness. Finally, he was to become a member. Shoo-Bo was a little frightened, but he didn't want the others to know that.

The gang members gathered by a fire. Blue Wolf, one long-time member, used metal tongs to hold a coin in the fire. Then he pressed the hot coin into the skin of Shoo-Bo's forearm. Shoo-Bo gritted his teeth so that he would not scream. He knew that the gang expected the imprint of the coin to show up on his arm. That would mean he was brave.

Gang Dress and Symbols

People often think of certain styles of clothing when they think of gangs. Today, however, there is no typical dress. Intensive police operations often have forced gangs to change the way they dress. For instance, gang members don't always wear baggy clothes. Gang dress may be harder to spot than that. For example, gang members may raise a pants leg or wear their cap cocked to one side.

Gangs and Violence

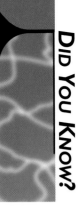
The "baggy look" has become widely popular in the United States. Even large department stores may sell clothes that people once associated only with gangs.

Members may mark their personal property with gang symbols. They also may mark their property with their gang moniker, or nickname. Gang members usually get monikers that fit their physical, personal, or mental traits. Some gang members get tattoos to show which gang they belong to.

Examples of Gangs

Los Angeles and Chicago appear to be the U.S. cities with the most gang activity. However, gangs can be found not only in large cities but also in smaller towns and even rural areas. Three types of inner-city gangs are West and East Coast, Asian, and Spanish-speaking gangs. These are not the only types but are common ones.

West and East Coast Gangs

The West Coast has a large number of gangs. Some of them have spread to other cities. For example, the Bloods and the Crips are two gangs that started in Los Angeles. They now are believed to have members in at least 45 Western and Midwestern cities.

East Coast gangs are found in New York, Boston, and other coastal areas. Gangs in Chicago often are considered to be East Coast gangs. West and East Coast gangs differ in many ways from one another. Yet experts note that West and East Coast gangs aften resemble one another in many ways. There is no one kind of gang.

Asian Gangs

Asian gangs are relatively new in North America. Some people believe that there is only one kind of Asian gang. This is a mistaken stereotype. In reality, families of gang members come from Japan, Thailand, Vietnam, Korea, and other places. Gangs whose families come from different countries usually are different from one another.

The stereotype about Asian gangs may affect the success of antigang programs. It is not useful to think of these kinds of gangs as based only on race (Asian). It is often more effective to understand the individual cultures that the gang members come from.

Spanish-Speaking Gangs

Like Asian gangs, Spanish-speaking gangs or gangs with a Spanish-speaking background are often different from one another. Spanish gangs may think of themselves as Latinos, Mexicans, Cholos (street family), Tex-Mex, or Guatemalan. Some Spanish-speaking gangs don't even consider themselves any of these.

Points to Consider

Why do you think the gang way of life attracts certain people?

What are some words you would use to describe inner-city gang members?

This chapter says all gangs are not the same. Why might it not be useful to think that gangs are all the same? Explain.

Do you think it's true that gangs don't dress a certain way? Why or why not?

Suburban gang members often have excess money.

Young people who join suburban gangs want to feel a sense of belonging in a group and to find acceptance.

Some types of gangs are delinquent, ideological, and occultic gangs or satanic cults.

Some suburban gangs perform acts of terrorism.

Chapter 3

Suburban Gangs

AUDRA, AGE 16

Audra's parents neglected her emotionally. They were rarely at home because of their jobs. They gave Audra anything she wanted, but she felt that they really didn't care about her.

Audra drifted into a group of other rich kids at school. She began to hang around with the gang most of the time. One of the members, a senior named Kal, once asked if Audra wanted to try some cocaine. She agreed to try a little. Within weeks, Audra was not only using cocaine but also selling it to other students.

For a while, belonging to the gang helped Audra feel good. However, she soon began doing more drugs. As she did, she began to regret ever joining the gang.

Some suburban or wealthy gangs are found in big cities. They usually have no connection, however, with inner-city gangs.

A New Kind of Gang

Gangs are increasing in wealthy suburbs in the United States. Like young people in inner-city gangs, people usually join suburban gangs for a sense of belonging. They may have parents who are rarely at home or who seem not to care about their children. Alcohol or other drug use or physical or sexual abuse may have occurred at home.

Types of Suburban Gangs

Suburban gangs are sometimes known as sets. They may be divided into three types—delinquent, ideological, and occultic gangs or satanic cults. Each type may be involved in criminal activity.

Delinquent Gangs

Delinquent gangs have a desire for money and power. These gangs are involved with such criminal activity as assault, theft, burglary, and drug trafficking. This type of suburban gang is considered most likely to grow the fastest during the next few years.

Ideological Gangs

Ideological gangs base their behavior on a specific set of beliefs. An example of an ideological gang is skinheads or white power gangs. Members of these gangs may shave their head closely. They usually believe that the white race is better than all others. These groups often hate people of other religions, countries, or races.

Skinhead groups exist in European countries such as Germany and Poland. Groups in these countries are believed to have inspired similar gangs in North America.

Myth: A gang and a cult are the same thing.

Fact: A cult is a separate group of people who follow a leader. The group usually follows some sort of religious belief. The leader usually demands unquestioning loyalty to her or his beliefs.

Occultic Gangs and Satanic Cults

Occultic gangs believe in supernatural powers. The illegal activities of these gangs usually are limited to drug trafficking. However, some occultic gangs have committed murders. Some similarities exist between these gangs and cults, which are groups with an unusual religion or belief. For example, cults and occultic gangs usually have a strong leader who promotes an unusual belief system.

Satanic cults have formed in some suburban communities. In many cases, members of these cults do not have close family ties. However, they often do have money to spend. Recruits to these groups usually do not have many friends. Cult members become friends for new recruits.

Leaders of satanic cults lead members to believe that an evil spirit will give them special powers. The leaders in some satanic cults use this promise of power to control new recruits. The leaders often use new members to get more money from drug sales for the cult. Sometimes satanic cult members take part in ceremonies that involve killing animals.

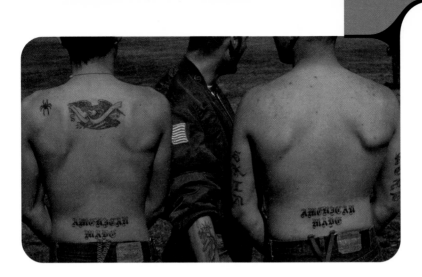

Suburban Gang Identity

Many suburban gangs move around and have no sense of territory or turf. One exception is delinquent suburban gangs that operate in areas where they can steal and sell illegal goods.

Suburban gang members come and go from the gang. They have few pressures to remain in the gang. That is, they usually are not members of the gang for life, and membership doesn't last for generations. Many people leave the gang to take jobs or to go to college.

Members of suburban or wealthy gangs often use identification that is not easily visible. Part of the thrill for some wealthy gangs is having concealed identification such as a tattoo or certain jewelry. This helps members to remain invisible to others who aren't in the gang.

One in eight suburban teens reports having carried weapons to school or on the street.

Violence That Isn't Predictable

Violence from suburban gangs is random. It usually cannot be predicted. These gangs usually do not meet in well-known or familiar territory. This makes it more difficult for police to identify and track suburban gang members.

Because suburban gangs often have money and education, they may be capable of terrorist activities. A few individuals have learned to make bombs on their own. Wealthy suburban gangs have made many bombs.

Points to Consider

Do you agree that suburban gangs are a new kind of gang?
Why or why not?

What do you think are the main differences and similarities
between inner-city and suburban gangs? Explain.

What would you do if someone invited you to join an
occultic gang?

Which type of suburban gang do you think is hardest for the
police to track? Explain.

Gang graffiti causes fear as well as property destruction in a neighborhood.

Innocent people, including the family of gang members, are often victims of gang violence.

Gangs in schools can create an atmosphere of fear and hostility.

Young people join gangs because the life looks appealing. They also may join because they think this is a way to protect themselves and their family.

Chapter **4**

The Effects of Gang Violence

In some areas, the number of acts of gang violence is large. For example, researchers interviewed 4,000 young people in Rochester, New York; Pittsburgh; and Denver. About 30 percent had been a gang member at some time. This 30 percent had been involved with crime such as drug dealing. In one Chicago neighborhood, 300 shootings were reported during one weekend. Fourteen people were killed. Twelve of those killings were believed to be gang related.

Not all graffiti is gang graffiti. Some people called taggers use graffiti as an art form. However, without permission to paint something, the tagger's graffiti is vandalism and is illegal, just like gang graffiti.

The physical effects of gang violence may include graffiti, murder of intended or accidental victims, or school disruptions. Other effects are expenses to society and the growth of gangs. Fear is an emotional effect of gang violence.

Graffiti Affects Neighborhoods

Gang violence can have many effects on a neighborhood or city. One result is graffiti. Gangs may use graffiti to mark their territory. They often believe this shows their power. Graffiti may appear on buildings, mailboxes, public walls, sidewalks, or nearly anywhere. Because it damages property, gang graffiti is a type of vandalism. It also is a strong visual reminder that neighbors have something to be concerned about. When gang graffiti is visible, no one is safe.

However, in a way, graffiti can be useful. It helps authorities track gang growth. It gives them information about gang membership. It helps them track connections of gangs to other areas or cities.

Other Vandalism

Graffiti isn't the only kind of vandalism that gangs commit. For example, some drive-by and other shootings are a form of vandalism. Sometimes drive-by shootings are aimed at houses or other property. The shooting is not intended to hurt anyone. However, the owners are left with damaged property.

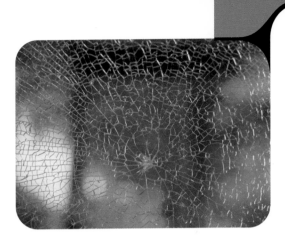

Sometimes gang members destroy public property such as parking meters, bus stalls, or lighting fixtures. Gangs often feel society doesn't respect them. They may feel that destroying property is a way to get back at society.

MAE, AGE 15

Mae was a member of the Evil Witches. One night she was out cruising with her crew. As they passed some boarded-up houses, one older member handed Mae a gun. She told Mae to hit the front door of one house.

As Mae fired, she saw an old woman walking nearby. She recognized the woman as Mrs. Wills, Mae's baby-sitter from when she was little. As the shot hit the door, Mrs. Wills screamed and tried to run. She was not hurt, but Mae could hear her sobbing as they drove off. Mae felt bad because Mrs. Wills had always been nice to her.

Harm to Victims, Families, and Witnesses

Murder and assault with guns are deadly effects of gang violence. These crimes may happen during drive-by shootings of homes, cars, or people. People are sometimes victims because they happened to be wearing gang colors.

Retaliation, or one gang getting back at another, is the cause of much gang violence. Most of this violent gang activity occurs in public places or at gang members' homes. Victims of fights are most commonly members of other gangs. Sometimes, however, families of gang members and other people may be hurt. Families regularly may see their children or siblings killed, injured, jailed, or using drugs. The grief families feel about a gang member's life is often unbearable.

Gang violence also can affect witnesses, who may feel trauma. This severe emotional shock may cause witnesses to feel afraid or helpless. Witnesses who see someone die may have double trauma. They must deal with both the violence that caused the death and the death itself.

Costs of Gang Activities

Gang activities can have financial and emotional costs. Gang activities such as robbery, auto theft, and arson can cost innocent people money. Their personal property may be gone or damaged beyond repair. Sometimes people spend money to protect themselves with extra locks or security systems. They might normally spend this money for other important needs. Sometimes people buy guns for protection, which may only increase the possibility of violence.

Gang activities also are emotionally costly. For example, innocent people may live in fear as a result of gang crimes. Often they feel as if their privacy has been invaded. They may be afraid to leave their home.

The Effects of Gangs on Schools

The presence of gangs and gang activities can affect schools. One effect is an atmosphere of fear for both students and teachers. For example, in one survey, 15 percent of the students said that their school had gangs. About the same number said that gang members had threatened teachers. For some people, school might be one of the few safe places in their life. When students can't learn because of gang activity, they have experienced another form of violence.

Gang activities in school also take teachers' time. Teachers must give attention to gang activity. This cuts down their teaching time and prevents other students from getting the most out of school.

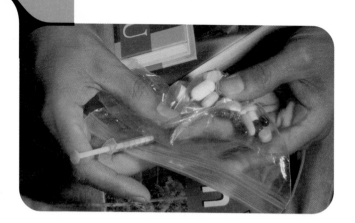

Authorities believe that a school with gang activity must take special safety measures. For example, many schools have installed metal detectors or hired guards. The money spent on these measures might be used for other activities. Such activities might keep some young people from joining gangs.

Attracting New Gang Members

Gangs like to recruit young people to be new members. Some gangs approach children as young as five or six years old.

Some gang activity attracts new gang members. For example, gang crimes may involve selling drugs or guns. Money from these sales might be used to buy clothes, music systems, or elaborate guns. These showy purchases sometimes attract others to the gang. They give the false impression of success.

Some young people are easy targets for the gang way of life. The cars, clothes, guns, and music systems may impress these young people enough to join. The gang's power spreads as these new members join.

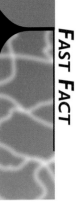
Authorities estimate that in cities with established gangs, about **74** percent of gang members are adults. In other cities, however, most active members are estimated to be under age 18.

Many young people in gang areas believe they will be safer if they belong to a gang. They believe the gang will protect them and their family. Some people join a gang because they are afraid not to. Often, however, the opposite happens. The new members and their family are in even greater danger of violence. They may become targets of rival gangs. New members may be arrested and put in prison. Instead of feeling safer, most gang members end up living in constant fear.

Points to Consider

How do you feel when you see graffiti?

How do you think vandalism affects a community?

The book mentions a few costs of gang violence. Name some other costs.

In what other ways do you think gang violence affects innocent people?

Leaving a gang can be hard. Many people believe that gangs often get revenge on members who try to leave.

Some people successfully retire from gangs for good jobs or a chance to go back to school.

Keeping a young person from ever joining a gang is the key to decreasing gang membership.

Many programs have been successful in helping young people avoid joining a gang.

Resilience can help youths avoid or leave gangs.

Chapter **5**

Reducing Gang Membership

Leaving the Gang

Leaving a gang can be hard for young people once they are
members. Many gang members feel that they just can't live
without the gang. They may fear they won't have friends outside
of the gang. They may be frightened that they or their family will
be killed or injured. Some gangs regard members who leave as
disloyal. The gang may seriously threaten a member into staying
in the gang. The gang may fulfill the threats by killing or injuring
a former member or someone in his or her family.

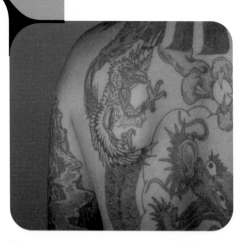

However, some gangs won't threaten members who leave unless those members know too many secrets about the gang. Gangs seem to respect some reasons for leaving. For example, having children or being on probation are often acceptable reasons to retire. Sometimes gang members can simply fade out of the picture. A deep religious belief may help a member leave.

Even though leaving the gang can be frightening and hard, help is available for members who want to leave.

ENRIQUE, AGE 17

Enrique was a member of the Pistoles gang. He had never actually killed anyone himself. However, he knew that could happen if he didn't die first. Enrique's family wanted him to leave the Pistoles.

One day, Enrique secretly went to the police and described plans for an attack involving the Pistoles. Soon, three of his fellow gang members were arrested. Enrique and his family quickly moved to another town. It seemed like the only way for Enrique to get out of the Pistoles. It also was the only way he and his family could be safe. Enrique regretted that he caused problems for many people by belonging to the gang. He was relieved to be out of the Pistoles.

Help for Leaving the Gang

Programs are available to help youths who want to find a place outside of the gang. With the help of these programs, many young people who have left gangs have participated in their own success. These agencies ask gang members to help in planning a strategy that will redirect and improve their life. In some cases, vocational schools and business leaders team up to provide new options for job training and opportunities.

Tattoo removal programs can help people to leave gangs, too. A tattoo can be a visual reminder of someone's past. Getting rid of the tattoo can provide a chance for a new beginning. Several state and city agencies offer free tattoo removal for gang members. For example, San Jose, California, has the Clean Slate Program. The program provides tattoo removal and increases opportunities for education and good jobs for gang members.

In Miami, ASPIRA Associates has established youth clubs in middle schools and high schools. They offer the support that teens might otherwise seek in gangs.

Preventing Gang Membership

Most experts believe that the key to decreasing gang membership is to keep youth from joining in the first place. Positive opportunities can make joining a gang less attractive. Programs that help youths keep from joining gangs typically use one or more of the following methods:

Find ways to give young people a sense of power and control in their life.

Teach anger-management skills to individuals or groups of young people.

Help young people understand what true respect is and how to get it.

Help young people understand what it's like to be a victim of violence.

Counsel parents and caregivers to help them improve communication and resolve conflicts in their family.

Hold community meetings with counselors, police, school administrators, social workers, and business leaders. These groups join together to increase opportunities for better jobs and protection from violence for young people.

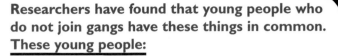

Researchers have found that young people who do not join gangs have these things in common. These young people:

Enjoy communicating with others

Think before they act

Have a high sense of self and personal responsibility

Believe they can make a positive change in their environment

Are flexible and learn to solve problems well

One program that educates kids about gang membership is Gang Resistance Education and Training (GREAT). The Phoenix Police Department teamed up with the U.S. Bureau of Alcohol, Tobacco, and Firearms. Together they created the first gang education program taught in neighborhood schools. GREAT has taught thousands of middle school students all over the United States about gang involvement. GREAT helps youth and police officers to get to know each other.

Students who are trained in GREAT tend to get along better with other people, including their parents. Generally, these students are more determined to succeed in school than those without the training.

In Philadelphia, the House of Umoja offers gang members a temporary home. The House of Umoja teaches gang members new job skills. It gets them involved in community service activities and eventually places them in jobs.

Resilience Helps

Learning to be resilient is a way young people can leave or avoid joining gangs. Resilience helps youths to overcome difficult odds. They can learn to bounce back from hard challenges with the help of a mentor. This is a supportive, caring adult with experience who accepts a youth unconditionally. Many mentors especially understand because they have thought of joining a gang. Some of them may even be former gang members.

Finding a mentor may be difficult. At the same time, it may be the most important part of leaving a gang. Mentors encourage young people to focus on their strengths rather than their problems. They teach youth to set and achieve realistic goals and take positive rather than negative risks. A mentor constantly expects a young person to succeed. Mentors help youths learn to live successfully without the gang. As a result, young people can learn to live with optimism, or hopefulness.

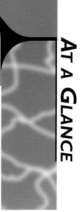
A group of volunteers in Dallas began a program based on resilience to keep youths from joining gangs. These volunteers worked with 400 young people who were likely to join a gang. Over a six-year period, none of the young people in the program joined a gang. The volunteers worked to match each youth with an adult who could be available whenever needed. Each adult volunteer regularly phoned his or her assigned young person. This support helped the youths to stay out of gangs.

Here are some keys to becoming resilient:

Get involved in school. Feeling successful in school can help a person to avoid taking negative risks.

Read. Effective reading skills can help a person adapt even to the most difficult problems.

Develop a sense of humor. It can help a person remain lighthearted when facing hard situations.

Learn to take initiative. Taking charge of problems works better than letting a situation control the person. Hope springs from successfully overcoming odds.

One Success Story

Tim McGee was the most feared gang member in Seattle in the early 1990s. He was in about 80 gunfights and once wounded a police officer. In 1992, Tim killed a man and was put in prison. One day, a minister named Reggie Witherspoon talked with Tim.

Witherspoon told Tim that he had presided over many funerals of gang members. He convinced Tim that it was not too late to turn his life around. Now Tim speaks with young people who may be at risk for joining gangs. Tim shares his firsthand knowledge of what gang life can lead to.

Rod's grandfather, father, and two brothers are members of the **ROD, AGE 18** Bullets gang. In fact, Rod's brother died in a gang shooting when Rod was seven. Everyone assumed that Rod would join the Bullets, too.

Always a good student, Rod wants to become an engineer. When Rod was 14, he decided never to be part of the gang. Rod's family thinks that he has betrayed them. He hopes that someday he will make them proud of him. Rod knows that if he ever has children, they will not feel they have to face the dangers of gang membership.

Points to Consider

How hard do you think it is for someone to leave a gang? Explain.

How might tattoo removal help former gang members?

Why do you think it is better for young people never to join gangs than to try to get out once they are in?

How resilient do you think you are? Explain.

What ways can you think of to keep young people from joining gangs?

More and better programs are being developed all the time to reduce or prevent gang violence.

Many states have increased penalties for crimes that gang members commit.

Cities have taken many measures, including curfews, to cut down on gang activity.

Schools have made changes to decrease the likelihood of gang problems.

Individuals can do many things to stay safe.

Chapter **6**

Avoiding Gang Violence

Experts agree that living in a peaceful atmosphere helps people to feel safe and valued. State and city governments, community organizations, and schools are developing programs to reduce or eliminate gang violence. Better opportunities for education, recreation, and employment can help prevent the growth of gangs. These positive steps help to create a safe, peaceful atmosphere for everyone.

The U.S. Department of Justice has a program called Executive Office for Weed and Seed. This antiviolence program includes community policing, law enforcement, crime prevention, and neighborhood fix-up.

States Take Action

Many states have passed legislation that may help curb the spread of gangs and gang violence. For example, the Governor's Commission on Gangs in Illinois helped increase the penalties for gang members who commit crimes. Illinois made it unlawful to force someone to join a gang or to prevent a person from leaving a gang. The laws protect victims of gang violence as well as people who provide evidence against gang members.

Other states have passed laws, too. For instance, California and Arkansas are among states that have increased the punishment for such gang-related crimes as drive-by shootings. Tennessee has a law that increases jail time if a person who commits a crime is a known gang member. In Nevada, gang members can lose personal property that has been used in gang-related crimes.

Success Stories in Cities

Cities across the United States have taken successful action to cut down on gang activities. Some cities have programs to provide alternatives for gang members. For example, a program in Seattle offers teens recreational opportunities such as team sports. The program also offers guidance to those who want more education. It offers employment services and interviewing assistance to youths who want to get away from gang life.

Many cities have successfully passed laws against cruising and other types of gang activity. They also have increased their investigations of drug trafficking and other gang crimes. These investigations have resulted in arrests and reduced gang activity. In many communities, curfews make it illegal for young people to be on the streets after a certain hour. The regulation of spray paint sales in several cities has decreased graffiti and other vandalism. Some cities even hold parents and caretakers responsible for the crimes that their children commit. Often housing projects, including those that government agencies regulate, remove residents who use guns.

Sometimes neighbors organize to prevent gang violence in their area. For example, people in the Phillips neighborhood of Minneapolis have organized to take back their streets from gangs. They patrol certain areas, report suspicious activities, and refuse to tolerate gang activities such as drug dealing. They have gotten the help of local businesses in their efforts.

Schools Can Help

Many experts believe that schools have an important role in helping students live without gangs or gang violence. More options for different school courses may help some students find enthusiasm for interests other than gangs. Students may work with mentors or peers to resolve specific problems. Schools can help parents and caregivers learn how to help their children avoid gangs.

Some schools let students meet in small groups to develop their own ideas for dealing with gangs. This allows students to share their hopes and dreams for a problem-free school environment.

Close monitoring in schools reduces the likelihood of gang fights and violent assaults. It also reduces the use and sale of drugs and weapons. Such monitoring makes schools safe for students and staff alike.

The city of Harvard, Illinois, bans people from wearing gang-related colors and symbols in public. Also, people cannot make public gang gestures or threatening sounds of any kind. As a result, almost all gang-related arrests ended within the first two years after the ban.

CLARE, AGE 17

Clare is the youngest of three girls. She loves her father and has always been special to him. When Clare was 12, her father volunteered to be a Big Brother to young boys who didn't know their father. He often spent Saturday afternoons watching ball games, flying a kite, or canoeing with a Little Brother.

Sometimes Clare resented her father's spending so much time with these kids. She wondered why he didn't spend that time with her. Then one day, Adam, who had been her dad's Little Brother for about a year, talked with her.

"I love my mother. She's great. But your dad has made me feel important. I know that I will always matter enough for him to listen to what I have to say. You're lucky to have a dad like that. And I'm lucky he's my Big Brother."

Clare agreed that she was lucky to have a dad like that.

Gangs and Violence

What You Can Do

Individuals also can help to fight gang violence. Here are some things that you can do to avoid or prevent gang violence:

Stay away from people who you know are in a gang.

Use safe methods to report all suspicious activity that might be gang related. For example, contact police instead of taking action yourself.

Avoid areas that are known as gang meeting spots.

Avoid walking alone at night, particularly in areas that are known or suspected to be dangerous. Stay in well-lit areas.

If you know someone who might become a gang member, ask a trusted adult for help. That adult may be able to direct the individual away from the gang.

Participate in or suggest starting a Neighborhood Watch program to protect your area from gang activity.

If you know that gangs wear certain colors or clothes, wear different colors or clothing styles. That way you may avoid being mistaken as a gang member.

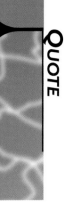

"Don't join a gang. You won't find what you're looking for. All you will find is trouble, pain, and sadness. I know. I did."—Stanley "Tookie" Williams, surviving cofounder of the Crips

Points to Consider

What recent methods have your city or state used to deal with gang violence?

If you were the principal of a school, what would you do to deal with gangs?

Who do you think is most responsible for reducing gang problems? Why?

Glossary

barrio (BAR-ree-oh)—Spanish word for neighborhood

delinquent gang (di-LING-kwuhnt GANG)—a suburban gang with a desire for money or power

extortion (ek-STOR-shuhn)—cheating people of money by frightening or threatening them

gangbanger (GANG-bang-ur)—a regular gang member

graffiti (gruh-FEE-tee)—drawing or writing on a public surface

hood (HUD)—a short term for neighborhood

ideological (i-dee-uh-LOJ-i-kuhl)—representing a specific set of beliefs

mentor (MEN-tur)—someone with experience who encourages a person who needs or wants guidance

moniker (MON-ih-kuhr)—a nickname

occultic (uh-KUL-tik)—relating to supernatural powers

recruitment (ri-KROOT-muhnt)—action to get a person to join a group

resilience (ri-ZIL-yuhnss)—the ability to recover from change or problems

satanic (say-TAN-ik)—having to do with evil

set (SET)—a common name for a smaller part of a larger gang organization

turf (TURF)—an area thought to be special or reserved for a gang

For More Information

Atkin, S. Beth. *Street Voices: Young Former Gang Members Tell Their Stories.* New York: Little Brown, 1996.

Gedatus, Gus. *Violence at School.* Mankato, MN: Capstone Press, 2000.

Miller, Marilyn. *Coping With Violence in School and on Your Streets.* New York: Rosen, 1996.

Nuñez, Sandra, and Trish Marx. *And Justice for All: The Legal Rights of Young People.* Brookfield, CT: Millbrook Press, 1997.

Useful Addresses and Internet Sites

Juvenile Justice Clearinghouse
PO Box 6000
Rockville, MD 20849-6000

Mothers Against Gangs
1401 East Thomas Road
Phoenix, AZ 85014
www.mothersagainstgangs.org

National Crime Prevention Council
1700 K Street Northwest, Second Floor
Washington, DC 20006-3817
www.ncpc.org/teens.htm

National Youth Gang Center Institute for
Intergovernmental Research
PO Box 12729
Tallahassee, FL 32317

Project: No Gangs
www.duila.org/project.htm
Information on gangs, gang awareness, and
gang graffiti

Tookie's Corner
www.tookie.com
The story of Stanley "Tookie" Williams,
cofounder of the Crips, and his plea for others
not to follow in his footsteps

Youth Crime Watch
www.ycwa.org
Information from youth-led nonprofit
organization on ways teens can work to reduce
crime and drug use in schools and
communities

Gang and Youth Contact Line
1-800-680-4264 Toll-free throughout British
Columbia

Index

Index continued

Date Due

JUN 2 9 2004			